Reviews

"Who knew that a simple turn of the dial on a daily ritual that all of us already partake in (well, hopefully all of us) can transform our lives? In Smash Your Comfort Zone with Cold Showers, Jesse Harless gives you what you might call a "not-so-obvious secret" that will boost your energy (almost immediately) while enabling you to defeat your anxiety and overcome any self-destructive habits. And it's significantly easier than you might think."

— **Hal Elrod, international best-selling author, The Miracle Morning**

"I love cold showers and take them regularly. In Smash Your Comfort Zone with Cold Showers, Jesse shares his inspiring story and how cold showers became a significant part of his success rituals. What I know about Jesse is he's driven to help you overcome obstacles in your path in order to live your best life."

— **Rob Dial Founder & Host of the #1 iTunes Podcast MWF Motivation**

"What you do on a daily basis will determine your success. Jesse lays out a clear path on how to get unstuck from your daily patterns that no longer serve you. I know cold showers work and I take them daily. Tell all your friends to read Jesse's book."

— **Steve Gill, Tony Robbins Master Business Results Trainer, Master Platinum Coach and Mentor Coach**

"What a gifted writer you are, Jesse! It had flow and is life-giving and bone chilling."

— **Jackie Stavros, Author of Conversations Worth Having and Professor, Lawrence Tech University**

"Jesse Harless's book, Smash Your Comfort Zone with Cold Showers, is for anyone looking to take their life to the next level and shift gears from fine to extraordinary. I was a skeptic of cold showers, but have learned from this book why cold showers are a powerful game-changer. As a recovering food addict, I have found the practice of cold showers to be highly impactful in changing my mindset, emotional state and recovery. This is a must-read for anyone who is eager and ready getting comfortable being uncomfortable in order to design and live out their best life, one cold shower at a time."

— **Julie Reisler, Author, Speaker, Podcast Host and Life Designer**

SMASH YOUR COMFORT ZONE
WITH
COLD SHOWERS

How to Boost Your Energy, Defeat Your Anxiety, and Overcome Unwanted Habits

JESSE HARLESS

www.SmashYourComfortZoneBook.com

Disclaimer

This book is meant to provide helpful information about the subject addressed and should not be used as a diagnosis, prognosis, or treatment recommendation. Please consult your healthcare provider or medical practitioner before starting any new health program or treatment. The author is not liable for any action taken by a reader based upon this information.

Contents

YOUR FREE GIFT

I want to gift you with my 30 Day Smash Your Comfort Zone Cold Shower Journal.

With this free journal you'll be able to list your 30-day goals, track your cold showers, and record your daily progress.

You can download your free gift here:

https://www.jesseharless.com/freegift

Acknowledgments

I want to thank Nick Wright for his never-ending quest to bettering his life and motivating me to a 30-day cold shower challenge.
I am forever grateful.

Foreward

In my book about the healing power of water, *Health$_2$0*, I missed out on one important aspect: That a cold shower could be a tool for overcoming unwanted habits and certain addictions. It took Jesse Harless and his own experience of multiple challenges and addictions – he will tell you about them, and they were not minor, believe me – to experiment and come up with his own theory: That a daily prolonged cold shower works in disrupting negative patterns and routines. He is living proof.

Jesse Harless is the first one to admit that much medical research is still needed – like a multi-centered, randomized, double-blind trial on a great number of people with addictions - to prove his concept. But how do you blindfold someone to the fact that he is standing naked under an ice-cold shower? And let's not fool ourselves: There will be no money for a study that uses cold water ... which comes for free (well, nearly for free) out of everybody's bathroom faucet. In the face of that, a valid scientific trial is highly doubtful in the foreseeable future. That's why Jesse's book is a godsend: It gives you a tool in your hand just when your desperation about your life's challenges might be sky-high.

Jesse Harless concedes that a cold shower is not the only tool you need in your toolbox to successfully step out of your comfort zone and tackle unwanted habits. He also tells you about some other tools he has used (and still uses) like a morning routine, journaling, goal-setting, affirmations, visualizations, and others. I am proud to count Jesse Harless among my friends and consider him my *water brother*. I wish his book a great run in the world, and I hope that many people in addiction recovery find their way to Jesse's book.

—Alexa Fleckenstein M.D.

Introduction: My Story

I wish I had known about cold showers sooner. My teenage years were plagued with fear, negative self-talk, self-doubt, addiction, and extreme social anxiety. I had a story I would constantly tell myself that people didn't like me, that they laughed behind my back and didn't respect me. I had an incredible fear of the opinions of others, and I rarely felt like a part of any group. I often engaged in addictive behaviors such as pornography and online gaming to deal with my emotions, fear, and anxiety.

I started freshman year of high school with enthusiasm, but midway through the year, I again felt disconnected and alone. By senior year, I was late to school so many times the headmaster set up an intervention, and I nearly missed graduating with my diploma. I felt that it took too much effort to show up for life. During those years, I would often spend four hours each night getting lost in a fantasy world on my computer. With the strong nudging of my mother, I got accepted into a small college in New Hampshire. For a short time, there was momentum and hope, but eventually, I started partying more than I was studying. Selling my books for pizza and weed didn't help either. I didn't last more than two semesters before I flunked out of college.

Even though I felt like a failure, I was determined to not let my life spiral out of control. I eventually got a job at Staples and took classes toward my real estate license. My dream was to sell properties along the seacoast and achieve financial freedom. I had read the book

Rich Dad Poor Dad and I was determined to escape the "rat race." I attended every real estate class and took copious notes. The last step would have been to take the real estate exam. But a few weeks before my exam, my father passed away from liver disease—a direct result of years of heavy drinking. Even though he lived in West Virginia and I had no relationship with him, his passing marked the beginning of a major downward spiral. The night my father died, I was introduced to cocaine. Thus began my serious addiction to heroin, cocaine, alcohol, and pain pills.

This spiraling went on for the next three years until ending abruptly. It was 2005, and I was facing time in federal prison due to my addictions. I didn't realize it at the time, but my fear of these consequences propelled me into discovering positive habits that would change my life.

Our darkest moments so often turn out to be blessings in disguise.

While awaiting trial I began journaling, reading and praying every day. I started exercising regularly and reciting daily affirmations. I joined a men's group that met at 6:30 in the morning every Wednesday. I also attended 12-step groups consistently. Focusing on my recovery became my number one priority.

Taking intense action and making a commitment every day to 'do the next right thing' paid off. The judge could see that I had turned my life around and I never had to spend a day in prison. I knew I had a second chance to change my life and show others what was possible.

Although my life improved dramatically over the next ten years of my recovery, I still struggled with self-confidence, addictions, procrastination, social anxiety, and low energy. I tried to incorporate more exercise into my daily routine by weight training five to six days each week. I began reading more self-help books, but I couldn't seem to apply any new principles for more than a month at a time. I was frustrated.

On a cold December night, a friend of mine suggested I take a cold shower every day for thirty days. I thought to myself, 'There's no way I can do this. I love my warm showers too much.' Besides, it was wintertime in New Hampshire. If I was going to have to admit to being addicted to steamy showers, I was okay with it. But my roommate must have sensed what would inspire me. Heading my protestation off, he strode upstairs to take his first cold shower. I was shocked by his decisiveness.

My friend padded back down the stairs and I saw that he had survived the stunt. I decided to try it, too. I turned the knob all the way to cold and turned on some music. I got myself pumped up and jumped in. The water was so cold it took my breath away, and I was in shock for the first thirty to sixty seconds. I stayed in that cold shower for a full five minutes.

I emerged, and would never be the same again. For the next three hours, I felt incredible energy and excitement—a level of energy I had never experienced before. I celebrated Christmas morning with a cold shower, which was my one-week mark. By *day thirteen*, it was snowing six inches outside and I still jumped in the cold water. When I hit the thirty-day mark, the end of my commitment, I decided to keep going. It was a no-brainer. That month provided me with unwavering confidence. Finally, I was taking consistent action and doing something good for myself. Somehow, this small, consistent act had returned on my investment in spades.

My ability to take on new challenges that had previously scared me began to mount. I started getting serious about overcoming social anxiety by using cold showers, EFT (Emotional Freedom Technique), and affirmations. My increased efforts in a new position at work helped me win a prestigious award that afforded me an all-expenses-paid trip to St. Moritz, Switzerland. Even in Switzerland, I did not miss a day of cold showers.

When I reached the one-year mark, I just kept going. Cold showers have become my uncommon recovery ritual as well as a lifestyle habit. I have spent many years of my life chasing highs from substances or fantasies. Now I chase natural highs like cold showers. I take them every morning and often take a second one in the afternoon if needed. It could be 90°F outside and sunny or 16°F and snowing. Regardless, I still take my cold shower.

Taking cold showers has changed my life dramatically. The intense interest from people I've told about my cold shower journey inspired me to write this book. My hope is that you will also begin to smash your comfort zone on a daily basis using the power of cold showers.

Part One:

Cold Showers:
My Uncommon Recovery Ritual

"Our biggest successes are born out of discomfort, uncertainty, and risk." – Gary John Bishop

Procrastination, perfectionism, resistance, fear, addictions, poor habits, and lack of energy prevent many well-intentioned people from making the necessary changes to create the life they want. When was the last time you made a resolution to change the way you eat, start an exercise program, or start something new only to quit when it got inconvenient?

In this book, I will show you how cold showers helped me to heal old wounds, reinvigorate my recovery, shut up the annoying mental chatter, and achieve results by implementing a cold shower routine. I'm excited to share the powerful, life-changing effects of cold showers with you. I'm going to help you solve your energy problem by laying out a step-by-step regimen for making cold showers a part of your daily routine to give you the edge you need to overcome any challenge.

Smash Your Comfort Zone is the principle behind the cold shower. The Cambridge Dictionary defines 'comfort zone' as *a situation in which you feel comfortable and in which your ability and determination are not being tested.*[1] Nothing ever grows in a comfort zone. The choices you make to do what you always have done will leave you stagnant, unfulfilled, and dissatisfied. When you consistently do things that make you uncomfortable and push you beyond your comfort zone, you inspire yourself and the people around you.

You begin to take charge of your life and smash your comfort zone by tackling the hardest thing upon awakening: a cold shower. I wrote this book for people in addiction recovery, but also for entrepreneurs, business professionals, salespeople, musicians, students, teachers, and anyone who wants to change their limiting beliefs and self-judgment; to overcome unwanted habits and surrender their procrastination. And I wrote this book for anyone who wants to retire their failure to commit. This book is for those who are looking to break through any self-imposed barriers. The result will be a life that excites you and helps you to thrive.

As a person who has spent the past few decades trying to overcome destructive addictions, I have read dozens of books and articles and tested countless theories about mindset and psychology. I could learn from my failures because I have extensively documented my journey to overcome social anxiety, fear, and negative behaviors that have baffled and shackled me for nearly two decades.

Cold showers will be a new experience for many of you. People might scratch their heads and question your sanity when you tell them about cold showers. If you take action and follow the suggestions in this book, you will be able to overcome old patterns that are holding you back, and I promise your life will never be the same.

Do it now! I don't want you to live with regret. Don't miss out on the power of cold showers because you think it might be uncomfortable. Growing is uncomfortable. Every day of my initial thirty-day cold shower challenge, I resisted it. I had to ignore my negative self-talk and do it anyway because I sensed this challenge was going to change my life.

The ideas outlined in the chapters of this book have produced long-lasting results for me. Each chapter will provide insight into what I learned and what I gained after taking cold showers for the last two and a half years—and I don't plan on stopping anytime soon. Expect to begin developing better habits that will improve your health, change your mindset, help you overcome obstacles, and begin to create the life you didn't even dare to dream up.

It's time to challenge your greatest fears and experience what's on the other side. No more running your life on autopilot. Let's break the unproductive routines of your daily life that are holding you back.

Chapter 1
Why Cold Showers?

"You'll never find success until you change something you do daily. The secret of your success is found in your daily routine."

— John Maxwell

Cold showers have helped me break through many obstacles over the last few years, such as overwhelming workloads, stress, fears, progress in my recovery, anxiety, self-doubt, and low energy. But tackling these obstacles was not an easy task for me. I had to dig deep and push through many of the same challenges you will face when you want to play bigger and break the negative habits you have developed over the years.

Here were some of my thoughts when I first began taking cold showers: *No way, no way, no way. Life is hard enough as it is. I deserve to take a warm shower to relax and be comfortable. Besides, I might get sick if I take a cold shower every day. I can't afford to get a cold. Plus, I live in New Hampshire and it's winter time!*

Physical and mental discomfort scared me in the beginning. The cold water was uncomfortable when it hit my body and my mind screamed for relief. After only a few days, I began to notice a shift in my energy and mindset. The thirty days of the challenge came and went. Incredibly, I stuck with it. And now, approaching my third year of cold showers, it is still part of my daily routine.

So, why do I continue?

Most days, I wake up and feel like hitting the snooze button. Sometimes I feel overwhelmed by some negative thought or another, just as you might. But I had allowed the snooze button to have power over my day for too long. This is why a morning routine that includes cold showers is vital for my physical and mental well-being. Combining cold showers with a powerful morning routine became the energy spark that changed my life.

Chapter 2
Being At Your Best

"The activities that you are most afraid of are the activities that can cause a breakthrough in your success."

— Darren Hardy

Here is how my daily cold shower routine works.

The first thing I do when I wake up is to set aside my negative thoughts and my impulse to hit the snooze button and sleep in. I make my bed, drink eight to ten ounces of water, take my plant-based multivitamin, brush my teeth, throw cold water on my face, and do three minutes of stretching. Next, I proceed with my morning routine which includes affirmations, visualizations, and gratitude journaling. The most powerful morning routine I have found is *The Miracle Morning* by Hal Elrod. I would also strongly recommend reading *The Miracle Morning for Addiction Recovery* by Hal Elrod, Anna David, Joe Polish, and Honorée Corder to learn more.

At the end of my morning routine, I prepare my cold shower music and sync up to my Bluetooth speaker. Just thinking about the cold shower makes me feel the energy rise up in me. The anticipation of jumping under that cold stream is both terrifying and invigorating. I turn on the shower and crank the water cold. I hit *play* on my favorite music track, do some jumping jacks to raise my heart rate and get my blood flowing, pull the curtain, and jump in. It's time for a rapid shift in mindset and energy. The cold water is exhilarating. For the next five minutes, my plans for the day disappear, and I am completely immersed in the present moment. My breathing is deep the entire time. My mind is clear. When the water stops, I feel unstoppable.

Now it's your turn.

If you are having trouble getting outside your comfort zone, if you experience constant negative self-talk or self-judgment, or if you need the inspiration to start something new, try making cold showers a part of your daily routine. Your mind will try to talk you out of it. That's its job: self-preservation. After all, couldn't hypothermia kill you? But the fear of hypothermia might just be your mind trying to talk you out of the cold shower. In reality, you would have to be in water that is 32°F or colder for about 30 minutes to experience hypothermia, so you have nothing to worry about with a cold shower[1]. By taking a cold shower and ignoring the impulse to preserve your comfort zone, you are telling your mind who's in charge.

You have the power to choose your thoughts, the images you visualize, your actions and your behaviors. During my cold shower journey, I learned that my thoughts can be quite negative; my mind is always telling me what *not* to do. My mind tells me my goals are too big and overwhelming; that I should avoid conflict and challenges that will help me grow and walk away from discomfort and unfamiliarity. It tells me, "Don't do it!"

And how do I respond? I choose to ignore my resistance on a daily basis and take a cold shower anyway.

Cold showers have helped me to take action that counteracts unhealthy habits such as viewing internet pornography and excessive caffeine consumption. They have also helped me to face failure head on. I want the same thing to happen to you. I started taking cold showers as a challenge, not expecting anything in return. But this simple action transformed my inner game (mindset) and my outer game (habits).

Chapter 3
The Cold Shower Advantage

"We grow fearless when we do the things we fear."
— Robin S. Sharma

Before taking daily cold showers, I attempted to manage my fear, anxiety, resistance, and energy without much success. I journaled my progress, but nothing would stick. Eventually, I fell back into my old habits such as allowing a thought to enter my mind about how tired I was, or using Facebook to distract myself from things that needed to be done. If this describes your mental habits, keep reading.

If your energy is low, your results will be poor or mediocre at best. Unfortunately, we are only provided so much energy and willpower in a day. Managing your energy is essential to daily success. Most of us wish we could have unlimited energy. Although factors like age, sleep, nutrition, caffeine, exercise, and water intake can affect our energy, how we start our day plays a significant role. If you want an easy way to increase your energy and kick-start your day, take a cold shower first thing in the morning. A cold shower in the afternoon or after your workout will also help keep the endorphins—your feel-good hormones—rolling.

I want you to experience more energy. Energy is the most essential resource in our success toolkit. It took many years for me to realize that my unhealthy habits were robbing me of vital energy. These habits included not paying attention to what I ate, procrastination, drinking excessive caffeine, and sleeping in.

The secret I am sharing with you is that you can use the energy you obtain from a cold shower routine to tackle your unwanted habits and fuel your day. If you can conquer a five-minute cold shower, you can conquer anything. Cold showers build and maintain a mindset of resilience, which will keep you centered and focused in the face of adversity.

No matter where you are in life, there's always a higher level. To get to the next level, you need to decide that *now* is the time. My challenge to you is to start building simple daily habits that will help you reach your next goal. A cold shower is a simple but powerful habit. Once you have mastered this powerful habit, you can stack it alongside other success habits such as exercise, affirmations, and writing a gratitude list. Or, you could stay exactly where you are right now. You could put off taking a cold shower today. You could put off making those phone calls. You could put off going for that run or workout. You could put off writing thirty minutes every day to complete your book.

Taking cold showers gives you confidence in yourself—confidence you will need on a daily basis to have the courage to face your fears, no matter how big or small. This confidence will also help with anxiety, which is created in the mind when we obsess about some future event which might never come.

Many people spend money on pills, courses, and diets designed to elevate your energy levels. Cold showers are a faster, easier, and less expensive way to get the same results –not to mention the money you will save on your heating bill.

Cold showers have helped me during life-changing decisions, and now my goal is to inspire as many people as possible to start making significant changes in their lives. I understand what it's like to live in fear and to not let yourself shine. We often create prisons in our minds. We don't know or can't see what is possible for ourselves.

Sometimes it takes but a small shift, a habit, or a daily commitment to put us on the path to the success we desire.

Why do I get up every day and take a cold shower? I do it every day because I need to show up for life every day. Of course, my comfort zone and negative thoughts don't go on vacation. But they recede into the background. For those of you who are cringing at the thought of taking a cold shower, do not be concerned. You can do what's called a 'James Bond Shower' or 'Scottish Shower' by taking a warm shower as usual and then finishing with the last thirty to sixty seconds of your shower freezing cold. You can also take a contrast shower, where you alternate the water back and forth between hot and cold for a few intervals. **Just make sure you always end on cold**. In time, you can work your way up to taking a shower cold for a full five minutes.

When are you at your best? I take cold showers in the morning when I have the most energy. I love to tackle my toughest tasks first thing after a cold shower because that's when I feel most empowered. Find a cold shower routine that will work best for you. I will talk more about my cold shower routine in Part Three.

Chapter 4
Get Uncomfortable

"Life begins at the end of your comfort zone."
— *Neale Donald Walsch*

What are you avoiding that's uncomfortable? As humans, we tend to avoid pain and seek comfort and pleasure. We love to stay warm and cozy in our familiar routines. Feeling uncomfortable is not something we like. Putting ourselves out there in the world and being willing to fail is uncomfortable. The problem is that success lies outside our comfort zone. I recently signed up to run my first marathon even though I'd never run even a 5K race before. Running four to five days a week was uncomfortable, but it was necessary to reach my goal.

It's not easy to start taking cold showers on a regular basis, the same as any deliberate change in habit or behavior. Once you begin to take a daily cold shower and to continually push yourself, you get used to the discomfort. And we need discomfort in order to change. You begin to look forward to the discomfort because you know growth is inevitable.

A cold shower seems like a small change. But this small change, executed repeatedly over a period of time, will amount to massive change. Make it your life's mission to walk through the fear, discomfort, self-judgment, and insecurity, and the result will be endless growth.

Your daily cold showers will allow you to look fear in the eye, and to decide to actualize your goals anyway.

Part Two:

The Benefits

"I have an icy-cold shower every morning."
– Hugh Jackman

Why would the likes of Tony Robbins, Tim Ferriss, and Hugh Jackman all expose themselves to freezing cold water on a daily basis – not to mention James Bond? The bottom line: concrete benefits. Cold showers help improve mental, physical, emotional, and spiritual well-being. In this section, we're going to dive into the various benefits of cold showers. These benefits are mostly from firsthand experiences. To experience the full benefits of cold showers, I would recommend taking them for a minimum of thirty days. But you will experience many of these benefits within a few days of adopting the practice.

If you're anything like me, you usually don't do something unless it makes you feel good. You might be thinking, "How does taking a cold shower make me feel good?" You will have to experience it for yourself to know exactly what I mean. I'm confident you will grow to love the feeling of cold water as I have.

Chapter 5
Overcoming Unwanted Habits and Addictions

"Leaving your comfort zone behind is the only way to grow."
— Jesse Harless

During the course of our lifetime, we develop many habits along the way, some positive and some negative. In order to have a successful life, we need to develop positive habits we can perform on a daily basis.

Tackling unhealthy habits is tough, but not as tough as living with regret for the rest of your life. Taking a cold shower is the first step in facing your unwanted habits head-on. Do you keep repeating a behavior over and over again despite the negative consequences? I want you to think about the habits that cause you pleasure at the moment but have negative consequences later on that set you back. Write them down on paper. You can start to replace each unhealthy habit with a healthy one during your cold shower challenge.

How would your life be different if you could stop doing the things that are holding you back? As I mentioned earlier, energy and mindset play a massive role in your success. If you have energy and the right mindset, you can begin to tackle these unwanted habits. One of the most freeing experiences you can have is to overcome an undesired habit that has held you back for years.

I struggled with addictive porn use from the age of eleven. Around this time, high-speed internet was introduced to my area, which meant high-speed stimulation for my mind. I share this here because it has affected relationships with many people I love, and the topic does not get talked about enough in our society[1]. If you struggle with pornography addiction, try taking a cold shower the next time you are faced with a strong desire to watch. There are 12-step groups you can join, as well as professionals who are trained to deal with this affliction. You can also check out the book *Your Brain on Porn* by Gary Wilson to learn more about internet pornography and the science of addiction. With the help of daily accountability, the 12 Steps, close friends, meditation, yoga, exercise, and cold showers, I've been able to find recovery. But like any addictive tendency, I need to take it one day at a time.

I began overcoming other addictive tendencies and habits that were no longer serving me well by starting the day with a cold shower. My caffeine consumption was one malady that had baffled me for years. I tried stopping for a period of time, but I would always go right back. After I finally did stop my caffeine use entirely two years ago, I started having less anxiety and more energy than ever before. The process of taking control of all aspects of your life generates enormous momentum. You can use this momentum to create the life you truly want and deserve.

Since starting cold showers, I have been able to quit caffeine entirely. This might not seem like a big deal to you. But for me, it was huge. For seven years I drank two Red Bulls a day. I would keep a case of Red Bull in my trunk at all times. I *had* to have a Red Bull before work and another after lunch every day, and I didn't realize it was a problem until my anxiety started to increase. I would often convince myself that something else was causing my anxiety and low energy levels. Eventually, I became acutely aware of my body's needs and had to take a hard look at my caffeine consumption. It was not the amount of caffeine that was the problem – it was the dependence and damage the drug was causing to my mental health. Maybe for you it's something else – Facebook? Sugar? Sun tanning? If it's hurting your vitality and well-being, it's good to have self-awareness.

About four months into my cold shower challenge, I began to eliminate caffeine starting with the biggest offender first: Red Bull. I continued to drink coffee instead. I eventually eliminated coffee and began drinking 1 cup of black tea only. Then, on a trip to California, I drank a cup of green tea and decided it was time to let go of caffeine for good.

On the last day of the trip and on my second day without caffeine, I began to have terrible headaches that lasted the entire day. I had always feared what would happen if I didn't have my Red Bull or coffee. How would I cope? The truth was, my withdrawals only lasted about a week and I've never looked back. And now I know that headaches are less likely if you don't go cold turkey on coffee, but slowly wean your way off over time.

What was the result of quitting caffeine? My anxiety has plummeted, my energy levels are higher than ever before, and when combined with cold showers, healthy eating, and new positive habits, I feel the best I have ever felt.

My point in sharing this story is not to scare you into quitting your harmless one-cup-of-coffee morning routine. The point is to show you the power of cold showers. Taking a cold shower every day gave me the confidence to eliminate a dependence which I had for over a decade. What will you tackle during your first cold shower challenge?

Chapter 6
Mindset

"Focus on where you want to go, not on what you fear"
— Tony Robbins

There is a conversation occurring all day and all night in one's mind. Sometimes the conversation is helpful, but other times it is detrimental. Our mind will tell us to wait until conditions are perfect before taking action, or that we can't handle the task set before us. This is, of course, not true. It's important to remember that *we are not our thoughts.*

What you focus on expands. You can start to train your mind to focus on thoughts that build up your confidence and empower you to act on your affirmations. When I'm not singing during my cold shower, I am repeating powerful affirmations. I will say things like, "I'm a force for good who's impacting many people's lives"; and, "I take one hundred percent responsibility for my life"; or, "I deeply and completely love and respect myself." By the time my favorite song is nearing its end and my cold shower is complete, my mindset is more positive, resilient, and ready to tackle my goals for the day. You can laminate your affirmations and hang them in the shower. Because some of my greatest ideas come during a cold shower, I have recently purchased Aqua Notes to be able to write them down.

Your mindset is a key component to daily success. Strive to develop what Dr. Carol Dweck calls a growth mindset. Carol states, "Individuals who believe their talents can be developed (through hard work, good strategies, and input from others) have a growth mindset."[1] Try asking yourself after every situation, "What's great about this?" Making cold showers a part of your daily routine is a great way to develop mental toughness.

Bonus Tip: Before your next big appointment, interview, or speech, repeat your affirmations in the mirror just before taking a cold shower.

Chapter 7
Increasing Self-Discipline

"You can't grow in life if you don't push yourself."
– Benjamin Hardy

Besides mindset, self-discipline is one of the most important aspects you can master. If you want to start making changes and celebrating results, it begins with self-discipline.

If you want to change poor habits or produce optimal results, you must have the self-discipline of daily action. Cold showers are a great way to start this process. You may think it's extreme. Well, let me ask you two questions:

Will you go to any lengths to achieve the life you want?

Or will you let comfort and familiarity get in the way of your vision and goals?

To the second question -- of course not. You wouldn't still be reading this book if that were the case.

Making cold showers a ritual will give you the discipline to conquer other areas you want to improve. Do you procrastinate? Jump in a cold shower and get going. Are you putting off finishing your degree, running your first 5K, or asking someone special on a date? Do it now. Are you not wanting to take a cold shower because it's twenty degrees outside and you deserve to relax? Do it anyway! Nobody deserves to slump through life and never self-actualize.

Taking cold showers on a daily basis takes self-discipline in the beginning. But eventually, it becomes a habit, like brushing your teeth. You stop thinking about it. You just do it because you know it's good for you. Self-discipline is rewarding and you can reap the benefits by practicing it every day in every area of your life.

Chapter 8
Increasing Self-Confidence

*"The greatest gift you can give somebody
is your own personal development."*

— Jim Rohn

Self-confidence is something that needs to be continually harvested. I don't always have the confidence to do what needs to be done on a daily basis. What has built my self-confidence is seeing progress and experiencing real results. When I was younger, people thought I was shy because I was so quiet. The truth is I had a ton of things to say, I just didn't have the confidence to say them.

One way I increase my self-confidence is by consistently taking cold showers and following it up with an action that scares me. Gail Goodwin, the creator of Inspire Me Today®, states, "If you're not scared, you're not playing big enough." If I have the confidence to jump in a cold shower even when I don't feel like it, I empower myself to take other actions I don't feel like doing.

"Do one thing every day that scares you."

As I write these words, I have just surpassed day 1000 in a row of cold showers. I have become more self-confident as a result of taking daily cold showers and getting outside of my comfort zone. Last August, I left my 9-5 job in order to start my own business and pursue my purpose. My hope is that you if you desire to do something big that scares you, but don't have the confidence to do it, you'll challenge yourself to take cold showers. Whether it's for seven days, thirty days, one year, or more, you *will* experience more self-confidence and build self-esteem as a result. Taking cold showers for even a few days will teach you what an optimal life could be like.

Chapter 9
Facing Fear

"Feel the fear and do it anyway"
– Dr. Susan Jeffers

I had a fear of taking my cold shower, but I did it anyway. Now I know cold showers can help reduce our daily fears. I'm not talking about fears that keep us from danger or ones that come from actual phobias. I'm talking about everyday fears such as the fear of failure, fear of success, fear of not being enough, the fear of feeling less than, or fear of discomfort. These are the things that we tell ourselves that are simply not true. What I've come to find is that fear can be a compass. For example, if I walk towards my fear of failure, yes – something, amazing will be on the other side. If I walk toward a bear or oncoming traffic – not so much. What lies on the other side of the fear of taking a cold shower?

FEAR = Face Everything And Rise. Fear can be a motivating factor because we can use what we are afraid of to motivate ourselves to change. Cold showers alone won't overcome fear. You will have to take action and face your fears to see results. Jack Canfield stated, "Everything you want is on the other side of fear." We need to commit to doing the things we are afraid of the most if we want to achieve our goals. When I was asked to speak on stage in front of 400 people, I was terrified. About an hour before my speech, I recited my affirmations in the mirror and took a cold shower. My nerves went from a level ten down to about a level three, and I was able to give my best on stage. The more we run toward our fears, the more success we will experience. Avoiding actions that can help us grow and staying in our comfort zone is the most dangerous place for us to live. Cold showers in the morning are a great starting point for tackling our daily fears.

Chapter 10
Conquering Anxiety

"Move out of your comfort zone.
You can only grow if you are willing to feel awkward
and uncomfortable when you try something new."
– Brian Tracy

One of my greatest struggles in life has been the fear of being negatively judged by other people. I've battled this social anxiety since middle school. In high school, my social anxiety became so bad that I stopped eating in the cafeteria. I've dealt with debilitating social phobias even during my years in recovery from drug and alcohol addiction. Just going to the supermarket seemed impossible at times. I could not leave the house. In 2015, I made it my mission to overcome my social anxiety.

By continually changing my mental state with the help of cold showers, I am able to show up differently in the world. I now put myself in situations that in the past would have produced tremendous tension and anxiety. For example, I will sign up for events that will put me around people I barely know. I still feel anxious at times, but I'm able to stay focused and recognize that I'm creating my own anxiety. Cold showers enable me to feel the anxiety and do the action anyway. It is a habit that has brought me from anxiety to confidence. Get in the habit of taking actions that will help you face your anxiety.

Chapter 11
Reducing Depression

*"One can choose to go back toward safety
or forward toward growth.
Growth must be chosen again and again;
fear must be overcome again and again."*

— *Abraham Maslow*

Because of their mood-elevating effect, cold showers can help with depression.[1] Having personally experienced depression for over ten years, I have tried various treatments. I have done a lot of work on myself in order to be able to deal directly with my depression. I even worked with a clinical therapist for many years in the beginning of my recovery. I strongly recommend talking to a therapist if you are struggling with depression on a regular basis.

Why have cold showers been helpful in relieving mild depression? Taking a cold shower helps lift my energy and my mood to a state in which I feel ready for action. It's like a rush of dopamine. Or more specifically it's a rush of beta-endorphin and dopamine – feel-good hormones. According to Dr. Nikolai Shevchuk, researcher and molecular biologist, "Local and whole-body exposure to cold has been shown to induce production of beta-endorphin. This neurotransmitter is responsible for producing the sense of well-being and suppression of pain through opioid receptors." [2] I get my daily dose each time I take a cold shower. I have yet to be disappointed.

Dr. Peter Bongiorno, co-director of Inner Source Health, states, "I recommend patients with depression to use brief whole-body exposure to cold water in the form of a cold shower. Patients can start a shower at a comfortable warm temperature and slowly cool down the water over a five-minute period down to 68°F, at which point you can sustain for two to three minutes."[3]

I strongly recommend listening to upbeat, positive music before, during, and after your cold shower. I also recommend some mild exercise such as a few jumping jacks before taking a cold shower. By combining cold showers, positive music, and light exercise, you will put yourself in peak state that will improve your mood and help with depression.

Chapter 12
Spiritual Benefits
Becoming Present

"Life is available only in the present moment."
— Thich Nhat Hanh

I have found that one of the quickest ways to get into the present moment is by taking a cold shower. You can only be in the *now* in a cold shower. As someone who meditates every day for twenty to thirty minutes, I'm consistently turning my attention to the present moment. But I have struggled at times to fully engage the now. Taking cold showers has improved my meditation practice and outcomes.

When you jump into a cold shower, you immediately are welcomed into the present state. As the cold water hits your body, your thoughts become clear and focused on the task at hand. All of your challenges, worries, and tasks for the day are suspended for five minutes of pure chilly bliss. My primary focus is simply on washing my next body part. Immediately, my breathing becomes deeper, and I move a little quicker.

Staying in the present moment will help you see the big picture and not sweat the small stuff. Most people live in the past or constantly worry about the future. Developing a daily practice of cold showers will keep you grounded in the present moment. Learning to be present is a practice that can help shape the rest of your life.

Cold showers have helped me gain more self-awareness. I have become more aware of my thoughts and of the limitations I place upon myself. I practice deep breathing inside a cold shower and outside a cold shower. In our fast-paced world, it's not always about doing more. Sometimes it's about just being with our breath while staying in the present moment. Yogi Bhajan, who introduced Kundalini Yoga to the West, believed you should start every day with a cold shower. He stated that cold showers "open the capillaries and clear toxins at the deepest level of the body."[1] There are those, too, that believe that cold showers help to clear out your chakras, the energy centers in your body.

Chapter 13
Physical Health Benefits

"It is health that is real wealth and not pieces of gold and silver."
—Mahatma Gandhi

Cold water exposure is a form of hydrotherapy which uses water to treat illness and disease. Although you might have never heard of it, hydrotherapy has been around for thousands of years. From my own study of cold showers, the benefits are as good at age twenty as they are at sixty-five. Who knew water could be therapeutic? Academy award winning actress Katherine Hepburn took cold showers on a regular basis and lived until she was 96 years old. Bill Wilson, the founder of Alcoholics Anonymous, used hydrotherapy as part of his treatment for alcoholism. Japanese mountain monks practice what is called *misogi*, where they stand under freezing cold waterfalls (50°F and below) for ten minutes at a time for self-discipline, purification, and healing.[1]

There are undoubtedly many health benefits to cold showers, and with a quick search, you can find many studies on the benefits of the various types of cold therapy such as cold water-immersion and cryotherapy. I will attempt to explain the health benefits I've experienced, as well as the benefits through some of my research and by people who decided to take on my cold shower challenge. In her book "Health$_2$0: Tapping Into the Healing Powers of Water to Fight

Disease, Look Younger, and Feel Your Best", Dr. Alexa Fleckenstein says this about cold showers:

"Your immune system will work better, your mood will get a lift, your breathing will be less shallow, your muscles will feel stronger… As a whole person, you will feel better – and you'll be healthier."[2]

She adds:

"You'll feel alive and ready to tackle the stresses of your life, your hair will grow stronger, and you'll get colds and infections less often."[3]

In general, your overall physical and mental well-being will improve with cold showers.

Energy

Energy is one of the main reasons I take cold showers. Nothing is more important than energy. When my energy is low, I show up differently in the world. A cold shower increases energy, stimulates endorphins, and charges my senses. When we are full of energy, we attract good things into our lives. Cold showers are *activity number 137* in Dr. Johnny Bowden's book "The 150 Most Effective Ways to Boost Your Energy." Dr. Bowden states "A cold shower raises your metabolic rate, which can reduce fatigue and increase energy."[4] My most successful encounters with clients or when meeting new people are when my energy is elevated. I can't stress this enough. You need to make sure you are harnessing the energy necessary to produce the results you want. Cold showers are a sure-fire way to go from an energy level of six to ten out of ten.

Improved Mood

Cold showers make me feel like I've come alive. My mood instantly changes after three to five minutes in cold water. There are times when I'm in a funk, and I lack the motivation to complete my most important priorities for the day. I find cold showers to be the quickest way to change my mental state and improve my mood. When I first started taking cold showers, I experienced a sense of euphoria shortly afterward, like a runner's high. That effect has continued to happen even after hundreds of cold showers. Nothing gets me ready for the day better than a five-minute cold shower in the morning.

Stimulates the Sympathetic Nervous System

Our bodies have two big autonomic nervous systems – the sympathetic and the parasympathetic branch. To explain these complicated systems in simple terms: The sympathetic branch governs fight-or-flight mode, the parasympathetic handles the rest-and-digest mode. Together, these two systems reach your whole body, from the brain to all your glands, to the heart, lungs, and the digestive tract, and beyond. Many modern-day people live with plenty of food to eat, rest, and little exercise and movement. But it's important to focus on both action and rest in our daily lives. According to Shevchuk, "whole-body exposure to cold has been shown to activate the sympathetic nervous system, which is responsible for 'priming' the body for action, for example, during awakening."[5]

Dr. Brady Salcido, Founder of The Neuro Lifestyle, states, "I use cold showers in the morning to give my body a quick jumpstart to my day and let me be clear."[6] A cold shower in the morning begins a beneficial cascade of hormonal changes in your body, even involving sexual glands.[7]

Colds and Sickness

Being sick is one of the worst feelings. If I can find ways to avoid being sick, I will. I have been ill fewer than five days since starting cold showers in 2015. Even when I have been sick, I take a cold shower because it makes me feel better, although I take shorter showers. A study was conducted only a few years ago using hot-to-cold showers with 3,018 participants.[8] Researchers found a 29% reduction in sickness in those who took hot-to-cold showers for 30 consecutive days versus those who took normal showers. There was a 54% reduction in sickness if the participants combined cold showers with regular exercise.[9] At the end of this study, over 90% of the participants said they would continue taking cold showers. Bottom line: Cold showers reduce colds and sickness.

Muscle Soreness

Cold showers help improve recovery time after a workout. Many athletes use cold therapy after practice or training, and some bodybuilders will take cold showers after an intense workout. According to Juliff et al., "Hydrotherapy, specifically cold water immersion, can enhance recovery after both simulated and actual team-sport competition."[10]

I take cold showers after a long run or workout because I am less sore the next day. After I ran my marathon, my legs were very sore for the next three days. After each cold shower, my legs felt less sore.

Skin

One of the most noticeable benefits from cold showers is my skin. I have received several comments from people that my skin is glowing. I even feel my skin vibrating or pulsating after a really cold shower. Cold showers provide healthier looking skin. For years of my adulthood, my back was covered with acne, despite good hygiene. After several months of cold showers, my back cleared up.

Weight Loss

Cold showers may even help with weight loss. Cold water has been shown to improve your metabolism and increase brown fat, which is the healthy, energy-burning fat responsible for preventing obesity, diabetes and heart disease.[11, 12] In other words, the more brown fat you have the better. Brown fat keeps you warm when you are exposed to colder temperatures – that is why hibernating animals have a higher ratio of brown to white fat.[13] When combined with healthy eating habits, cold showers can be an effective way to tackle fat loss – mostly because it motivates you toward healthier eating habits. You have already done something great by taking a cold shower first thing in the morning. Why spoil it with a sugary breakfast?

The Doctor's Opinion

British born doctor Sonny Saggar, internist and founder of St. Louis Urgent Care, has been taking cold showers since he was a teenager. Naturally, he believes there are real health benefits to cold showers. According to Dr. Saggar, that list includes improved circulation, antidepressant, accentuated breathing, help with sleep, augmented immunity, improved metabolism, healthier skin, improved potency and fertility, weight loss, and improved lymphatic system.[14]

Dr. Saggar also points out that cold showers can even help save the planet because less energy is being used (in the form of gas and electric usage), which means less CO_2 and greenhouse gases in the atmosphere. That is a good thing!

A word of caution:

I would not recommend a cold shower if you are pregnant, or have health concerns such as heart disease or high blood pressure. If you have any doubts, please consult with a doctor before taking a cold shower.

I've suffered from Raynaud's syndrome for most of my life. Basically, my fingers become painful with constant exposure to the cold. Although some would not recommend cold showers, I still do it. In fact, I've noticed fewer symptoms of numbness and pain since the start of my cold shower journey when I'm in a cold environment. After a cold shower, I feel warmer throughout my day. This could have to do with the fact that cold showers can help to promote thermogenesis, an internal generation of body heat.[15] A cold shower does not leave you cold. As Dr. Fleckenstein put it, "Cold water stimulates your body to create heat by itself – and that is a healthy occurrence."[16]

Part Three:

My Cold Shower Process

"You get started by taking one small step, one action at a time"
– Darren Hardy

Are you now ready to change your patterns that are no longer serving you? I'm not advising that cold showers are going to change your life overnight. But if you give yourself a chance to get outside your comfort zone on a regular basis, you will begin to develop the mindset and resiliency you need to achieve all your goals.

What we do repeatedly, we become. Taking a cold shower every day reminds you of the person you want to become. Slowly you will take control of your thoughts and actions. Consistency is a critical element in seeing the real benefits of cold showers. A thirty-day cold shower challenge might be the domino that sets all others in motion.

Chapter 14
The Challenges

"You can't hire someone else to do your pushups for you"
— Jim Rohn

My cold shower journey all started with a challenge that would forever change my life. I want to provide you with the same challenge. There are times when we feel disconnected, fearful, and defeated. A cold shower challenge helps us live in the flow and operate at our peak potential.

Life has many challenges. How we show up to each challenge shapes our destiny. The cold shower challenge is about telling ourselves, "I won't quit,"; "I won't be defeated no matter what"; and, "Nothing can stop me." As we complete the one-month cold shower challenge, we tackle other challenges and obstacles with more energy, passion, zest, and confidence. Cold showers are a keystone habit that help to create other success habits.

You can choose any challenge that suits you. If you want to start with a seven-day challenge, you will still see results. I had results after my first cold shower—more energy, confidence, and motivation to do what I needed for the next several hours. Before you start the challenge, I want you to download my 30-day challenge spreadsheet to track your days and record your results. I also want you to answer these questions: What fear, obstacle, or adversity will I began to tackle during this challenge? What goal or project will I complete by the end of this challenge? What will my life be like at the end of this cold shower challenge?

The 7-Day Challenge

This is the 'easiest' cold shower challenge consisting of seven days. Here is an example of what might work for you: Start the first two days making the last thirty seconds of your shower cold (*James Bond Shower*). Over the next two days, make the last sixty seconds of your shower cold. Over the final three days, make it cold the entire time.

You will see results after one week of cold showers, so don't be concerned about the length of time. Once you get through a week of cold showers, make sure you celebrate your success.

Warning: You might get hooked!

The 30-Day Challenge

I strongly recommend you try cold showers for thirty days. Most of the people I've worked with stuck with the practice for thirty days and all of them experienced benefits. Some experts say it can take twenty-one days to create a habit. Taking cold showers for thirty days makes certain you are giving yourself enough time to create a lifelong habit.

For the 30-Day Challenge, you can break it into three sets of ten days if you'd like: Over the first ten days, make the last thirty seconds of your shower cold. Over the next ten days, make the last sixty seconds cold. For the final ten days, make the last two minutes cold. However, if you think you can take a shower cold the whole time for thirty days, more power to you (this is what I did). Find what works best for you. Just remember to always end your showers cold.

Please note that older individuals might have more difficulties with extended time under the cold shower. Ending each hot shower with a short cold one (twenty to thirty seconds) might be a good alternative. People who are sick might benefit from a short wash-down with a cold face-cloth.

Go to SmashYourComfortZoneBook.com
to download your free 30-Day Cold Shower Challenge Tracker Journal.

The 30-Day End-All-Hot-Showers-Cold Challenge

I realize some of you will be very happy to simply end your warm shower with a burst of cold —about twenty to thirty seconds. This challenge will have many of the physical health benefits we talked about. To experience all of the benefits, the bigger challenge of straight cold showers might be required.

The One Year Challenge

This is the ultimate challenge. It may seem impossible to take cold showers for a year, through all the seasons, including a harsh winter for some. But once you begin to experience a daily surge of energy and excitement for your day, this habit becomes a lifestyle.

Remember, you only have to take a cold shower one day at a time. The days will turn into weeks and the weeks will turn into months. Before you know it, you will have achieved this incredible goal and I guarantee you will be a different person as a result.

Chapter 15
Deep Breathing

*"Breathe. Let go. And remind yourself that this very moment
is the only one you know you have for sure."*

– Oprah Winfrey

One of my secrets to taking a cold shower is my breathing. In our daily lives, we don't often check in and see how we're breathing. If I had to guess, your breathing is shallow most of the time. Deep breathing increases oxygen to all organs, especially the brain, and relaxes the mind. I have suffered from asthma my entire life. Since starting my cold shower routine and practicing deep breathing daily, I have had a significant decline in asthmatic symptoms. I ran my first marathon without any problems with my breathing.

Before I get into a cold shower, I will begin to take deeper breaths. Once I'm in, I will continue to breathe deeply throughout the shower, particularly focusing on my exhaling. According to Dr. Fleckenstein, "When you exhale, your body is in relaxed mode."[1] Here is an example breathing exercise: Take a deep breath in through your nose for five seconds, hold it, and release it out through your mouth for at least five seconds. I keep repeating this throughout the shower, focusing on my breathing coming from my belly. Deep breathing helps me become very present and focused during a three-to-five-minute cold shower. Deep breathing will help you to relax during your cold shower.

Chapter 16
How Cold Does
My Shower Need To Be?

For most people, water that is below 70°F is going to feel cold.[1] When first starting out, try lowering the temperature between 70-75°F to get a feel for the cold. I typically reduce the temperature to between 57°F and 68°F for my cold shower. If your water is even colder, reduce exposure time. During my first cold shower challenge, my roommate would grab a digital thermometer and test how cold our showers were. We were being ridiculous, but we wanted to keep each other honest. You can purchase a basic thermometer to check your water temperature. If you live in places where your water is not as cold, prolong your exposure time. When I travel, the water temperature is not always as cold as back home, so I make sure I have the dial all the way cold.

Chapter 17
My Process

*"You don't have to be great to start,
but you have to start to be great."*

– Zig Ziglar

Now it's time to take your first cold shower. First, I will share with you my step-by-step process. The first step is to play my favorite cold shower music. Think about a song that gets you energized, or *pumped up*. One of my favorite cold shower songs is "Glorious" by Macklemore. Even though music is optional, I highly recommend it. You can play music from your phone or purchase a Bluetooth speaker to keep in your bathroom.

I perform ten to fifteen jumping jacks right before I enter the shower. Feel free to smile and laugh while you're doing your jumping jacks. Once I feel pumped up, I pull back the shower curtain and *jump in*.

As soon as I'm in the shower, I let the water hit the back of my legs; then I allow the water to move up my back and spine. I turn around and let the water hit the bottom half of my legs and slowly move forward hitting my stomach and chest. I am continually massaging my body parts as the cold-water hits. I begin to wash my entire body and rinse. **Remember to take deep breaths and keep moving!** The next part is washing my face and head. It's an endorphin rush for sure.

I keep my head under the cold water for a bit, but this is optional. Once I get my face and head in the cold water, I realize that I was making a big deal out of nothing. (In European Natural Medicine, you always start with your feet, hands, and face. Then, slowly go up your legs, and then your whole body.) I continue to turn the dial from cold to colder as I get used to the temperature.

The entire process can take anywhere from three to five minutes. However, I sometimes stay in a cold shower up to ten minutes. (Bonus points if you can find your favorite music track that's about five minutes long.) That way, you can jump out at the end of the song. Remember: Take your time with this. You don't have to take a ten-minute cold shower your first time. Your body knows what's best, so pay close attention to the way your body feels during and after a cold shower.

Warning: You might have so much energy and power that you rip the shower curtain off the rod at the end of your cold shower.

My energy continues to stay elevated as I get dressed for my day. My energy lasts all morning and I don't need caffeine. I don't need any substance at all. I let this good feeling set the tone for the entire day.

LET'S GET STARTED! Stop reading this book right now. Head to the shower. Today is the day! There is no better time than right now to begin your new journey—the journey of continually playing outside your comfort zone. I can't wait to hear about your results.

Accountability

> *"Change is hard. That's why we can't do it alone."*
> *— Russell Brand*

Try to get a friend, colleague or family member to do the cold shower challenge with you.

When I first started my thirty-day challenge, I had an accountability partner. When he stopped at the thirty-day mark, I just kept going. Eventually, there was no need for accountability. I knew the results were real. There are those, too, who only take cold showers occasionally for the purpose of changing their mindset, overcoming unwanted habits, or for an instant blast of energy.

If you can't find someone to share your journey with you, you can easily find someone in our Facebook group, "Smash Your Comfort Zone with Cold Showers." This group will offer support as you jump into the world of cold showers. It's there to keep you motivated during your first seven-day, thirty-day, or one-year challenge. You don't have to do this alone. But don't let the fact that you can't find someone stop you. As I mentioned earlier, cold showers can become a way of life. The Facebook community is there to share your successes with cold showers, overcoming unwanted habits, meeting the goals you've set for yourself, and provide encouragement.

Join the Facebook Group
"Smash Your Comfort Zone with Cold Showers".

Chapter 18
What Happens If I Don't Decide To Take Cold Showers?

"People love to hear good news about their bad habits."
— John A. McDougall

People will go to great lengths to protect their unhealthy habits and preserve their comfort zones. You can choose to continue doing the same thing you were doing before you read this book. But I have a feeling that if you made it this far, you are looking to try something different. I have tried to make clear the physical, mental, emotional, and even spiritual benefit of cold showers. You will have more energy, you will become a more disciplined person, you will gain mental toughness, you will be able to approach discomfort with more enjoyment, you will have a better immune system, healthier looking skin, and you may even shed a few pounds. Most importantly, you will start to view discomfort from a new lens. You will see that getting used to being uncomfortable is the key to long-term change and growth.

Chapter 19
Tranform Your Life

"You have the power to choose the rest of your story."
— Jesse Harless

You have a real opportunity to overcome unhealthy habits and live the life you thought was possible. Your Level Ten Life awaits you. It all starts with a decision. Make a commitment to yourself that you will start taking cold showers today.

I needed a kick start to my engine to tackle years of unhealthy habits. I have been able to replace several unhealthy habits with healthy ones using the methods mentioned in this book. This would not have been possible without a change in my physiology and mindset.

In his book, "The War of Art", Stephen Pressfield wrote "Most of us have two lives: the life we live, and the unlived life within us. Between the two stands resistance." Stop wasting time squandering away the hours of your life in comfort and resistance. During a thirty-day cold shower challenge I created on Facebook, many people were afraid of taking their first cold shower. But once they took action, they were hooked. Most of the participants continued taking cold showers.

If you have not done so yet, take a cold shower now. What do you have to lose?

Start with a two-minute cold shower and slowly work your way up to a five-minute shower. Or start with a warm shower and turn the dial cold for the last twenty to thirty seconds. I would love to hear about your progress, the habits you're changing, and how cold showers are helping you to become the best version of yourself. I believe the habit of a cold shower can help awaken the person inside you were meant to be.

You might be starting cold showers to encourage yourself to lose twenty pounds, go on your first date, quit sugar or dairy, or to start a meditation practice. Whatever your goal, start working on it today.

I hope you have now realized that cold showers are more than a boost of energy in the morning. Cold showers help you get used to discomfort, help you overcome your worst habits, and help you tackle your greatest fears.

Make sure you write down exactly what you want to accomplish during your cold shower challenge and record your daily progress.

When life hits you hard and you are faced with obstacles, just remember that you have tackled some significant fears and changed your daily habits by harnessing the power of cold showers. You thought it was impossible, but now you know you can do it.

About The Author

Jesse Harless is a person in long-term recovery as well as a Life and Recovery Coach, Facilitator, Speaker, Author, and Entrepreneur in Recovery. Jesse's journey of recovery began in 2005 when he was faced with multiple felony charges for his addiction to heroin, cocaine, and pain pills. Facing severe consequences for his actions, he started to change his daily habits and get serious about his recovery. He holds a Master's degree in Counseling from Rivier University. He is a Certified Professional Coach and a certified L.E.A.F. practitioner (Leading with Experiential Appreciative Facilitation). He is the founder of Entrepreneurs in Recovery, a platform to help people in addiction recovery reach their full potential. He works with several addiction treatment centers and programs in the Northeast where he facilitates his Appreciative Recovery Facilitation model. He currently helps run the Genius Recovery Facebook group with Joe Polish.

You can learn more here:

www.SmashYourComfortZoneBook.com

www.EntrepreneursinRecovery.com

www.JesseHarless.com

Facebook: JesseHarless22

Instagram:
@JesseHarless221
@EntrepreneursinRecovery

Email: Jesse@JesseHarless.com

Please join our Facebook group "Smash Your Comfort Zone with Cold Showers" for support during your cold shower journey.

I would be honored if you would review this book on Amazon. Thank you!

Endnotes

Chapter One

[1] https://dictionary.cambridge.org/us/dictionary/english/comfort-zone

Chapter Two: Being at your best

[1] http://www.coldwatersafety.org/ImmersionHypo.html

Chapter Five: Overcoming Unwanted Habits and Addictions

[1] http://time.com/4277510/porn-and-the-threat-to-virility

Chapter Six: Mindset

[1] https://hbr.org/2016/01/what-having-a-growth-mindset-actually-means

Chapter Eleven: Reducing Depression

[1] Shevchuk, Nikolai. (2008). Adapted cold shower as a potential treatment for depression. Medical hypotheses. 70. 995-1001. 10.1016/j.mehy.2007.04.052.

[2] Ibid.

[3] https://www.psychologytoday.com/us/blog/inner-source/201407/cold-splash-hydrotherapy-depression-and-anxiety

Chapter Twelve: Spiritual Benefits

[1] https://www.3ho.org/3ho-lifestyle/daily-routine/hydrotherapy

Chapter Thirteen: Physical Health Benefits

[1] Koshikidake, S., Hayes, S. K., & Faulks, M. (2015). Shugendo: The way of the mountain monks. Great Britain: Faulks Books.

[2] Fleckenstein, A., & Weisman, R. (2007). Health 2 0: Tap into the Healing Powers of Water to Fight Disease, Look Younger, and Feel Your Best. New York: McGraw-Hill.

[3] Ibid.

[4] Bowden, J. (2011). The 150 Most Effective Ways to Boost Your Energy: The Surprising, Unbiased Truth About Using Nutrition, Exercise, Supplements, Stress Relief, and Personal Empowerment to Stay Energized All Day. Gloucester, MA: Fair Winds.

[5] Shevchuk, Nikolai. (2008). Adapted cold shower as a potential treatment for depression. Medical hypotheses. 70. 995-1001. 10.1016/j.mehy.2007.04.052.

[6] http://www.drbradysalcido.com/hackvagusnerve

[7] Fleckenstein, A. (2018). The Benefits of Water Therapy for Sexual and Pelvic Problems. In Integrative Sexual Health (1st ed.). Oxford University Press.

[8] Buijze GA, Sierevelt IN, van der Heijden BCJM, Dijkgraaf MG, Frings-Dresen MHW (2016) The Effect of Cold Showering on Health and Work: A Randomized Controlled Trial. PLoS ONE 11(9): e0161749. doi:10.1371/journal.pone.0161749

[9] Ibid.

[10] Juliff LE, Halson SL, Bonetti DL, Versey NG, Driller MW, Peiffer JJ. Influence of contrast shower and water immersion

recovery in elite netballers. J Strength Cond Res. 2014;28:2353–2358. doi: 10.1519/JSC.0000000000000417.

[11] Mooventhan, A., & Nivethitha, L. (2014). Scientific Evidence-Based Effects of Hydrotherapy on Various Systems of the Body. North American Journal of Medical Sciences, 6(5), 199–209. http://doi.org/10.4103/1947-2714.132935

[12] Fleckenstein, A. (2014). The diabetes cure: *The 5-step plan to eliminate hunger, lose weight, and reverse diabetes for good!* New York: Rodale.

[13] Ballinger, M. A., & Andrews, M. T. (2018). Natures fat-burning machine: Brown adipose tissue in a hibernating mammal. *The Journal of Experimental Biology*, 221(Suppl 1). doi:10.1242/jeb.162586

[14] http://www.dhwstl.com/doctor-is-in-stl-blog/category/scottish-shower

[15] https://gettingstronger.org/2010/03/cold-showers

[16] Fleckenstein, A., & Weisman, R. (2007). Health^{2}0: Tap into the Healing Powers of Water to Fight Disease, look Younger, and Feel Your Best. New York: McGraw-Hill.

Chapter Fifteen: Deep Breathing

[1] Fleckenstein, A. (2014). The Diabetes Cure: The 5-Step Plan to Eliminate Hunger, Lose   Weight, and Reverse Diabetes for Good! New York: Rodale.

Chapter Sixteen: How Cold Does My Shower Need To Be?

[1] http://www.coldwatersafety.org/WhatIsCold.html#DifferentStrokes

Resources For Addiction:

SAMHSA – Substance Abuse and
Mental Health Services Administration
https://www.samhsa.gov/find-help/national-helpline

Genius Recovery https://geniusrecovery.com

Alcoholics Anonymous https://www.aa.org

Narcotics Anonymous http://www.na.org

Cocaine Anonymous https://ca.org

Heroin Anonymous https://heroinanonymous.org

Overeaters Anonymous https://oa.org

Codependents Anonymous http://coda.org

Gamblers Anonymous http://www.gamblersanonymous.org/ga

Sex Addicts Anonymous https://saa-recovery.org

Game Quitters https://gamequitters.com

Your Brain on Porn https://www.yourbrainonporn.com

SMART Recovery (Self-Management and Recovery Training)
https://www.smartrecovery.org

Al-Anon https://al-anon.org

Facing Addiction https://www.facingaddiction.org

Recovery 2.0 http://recovery2point0.com

Suicide Hotlines http://suicidehotlines.com/national.html
1-800-SUICIDE (800-784-2433)